D1507513

ZEBRAS

alex kuskowski

Consulting Editor, Diane Craig,
M.A./Reading Specialist

Sandcastle

An Imprint of Abdo Publishing
www.abdopublishing.com

visit us at www.abdopublishing.com

Published by Abdo Publishing, a division of ABDO, PO Box 398166, Minneapolis, Minnesota 55439.
Copyright © 2015 by Abdo Consulting Group, Inc. International copyrights reserved in all countries.
No part of this book may be reproduced in any form without written permission from the publisher.
SandCastle™ is a trademark and logo of Abdo Publishing.

Printed in the United States of America, North Mankato, Minnesota
062014
092014

THIS BOOK CONTAINS RECYCLED MATERIALS

Editor: Liz Salzmann
Content Developer: Nancy Tuminelly
Cover and Interior Design: Anders Hanson, Mighty Media, Inc.
Photo Credits: Shutterstock

Library of Congress Cataloging-in-Publication Data
Kuskowski, Alex., author.
  Zebras / Alex Kuskowski.
    pages cm. -- (Zoo animals)
  Audience: 004-009.
  ISBN 978-1-62403-276-9
  1. Zebras--Juvenile literature. I. Title.
  QL737.U62K87 2015
  599.665'7--dc23
                2013041829

SandCastle™ Level: Transitional

SandCastle™ books are created by a team of professional educators, reading specialists, and content developers around five essential components—phonemic awareness, phonics, vocabulary, text comprehension, and fluency—to assist young readers as they develop reading skills and strategies and increase their general knowledge. All books are written, reviewed, and leveled for guided reading, early reading intervention, and Accelerated Reader® programs for use in shared, guided, and independent reading and writing activities to support a balanced approach to literacy instruction. The SandCastle™ series has four levels that correspond to early literacy development. The levels are provided to help teachers and parents select appropriate books for young readers.

EMERGING · BEGINNING · **TRANSITIONAL** · FLUENT

CONTENTS

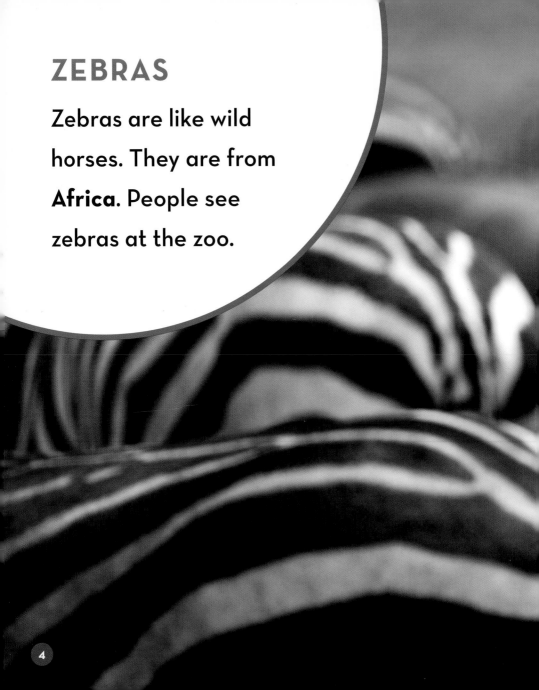

ZEBRAS

Zebras are like wild horses. They are from **Africa**. People see zebras at the zoo.

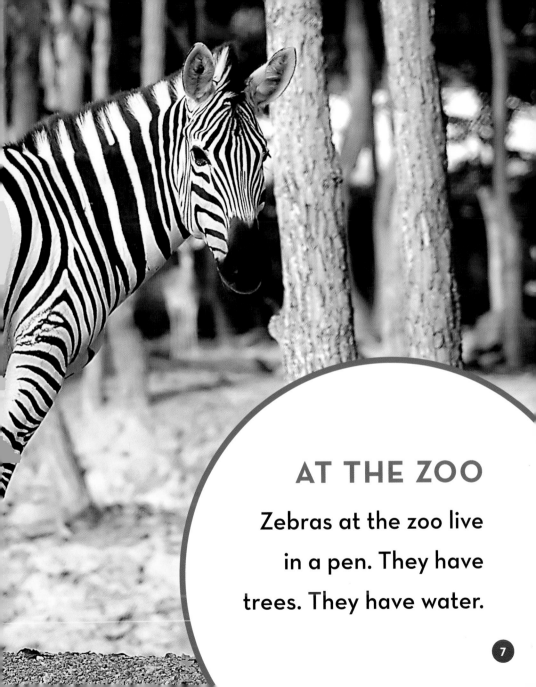

AT THE ZOO

Zebras at the zoo live in a pen. They have trees. They have water.

ZEBRA FEATURES

Zebras have black and white stripes. No two zebras have the same stripes.

Zebras live in large herds. They guard each other from danger.

Zebras need water
every day. They drink
at a watering hole.

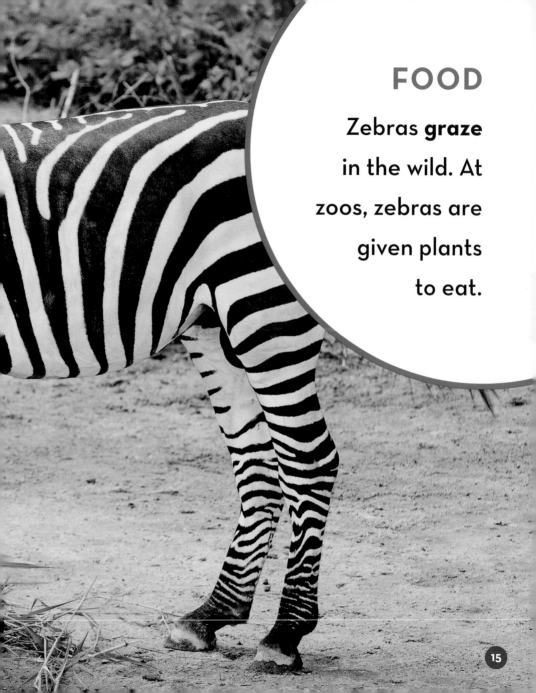

FOOD

Zebras **graze** in the wild. At zoos, zebras are given plants to eat.

ZEBRA FOALS

Young zebras are called foals. Foals stay close to their mothers.

ZEBRA FUN

Zebras **communicate** with each other. They make noise. They make faces too.

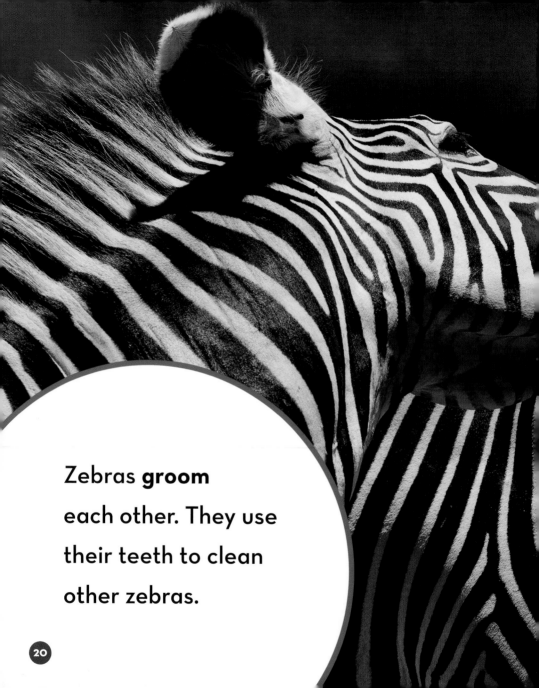

Zebras **groom** each other. They use their teeth to clean other zebras.

FAST FACTS

- Zebra foals can run one hour after being born.

- Zebras can run 35 miles (56 km) per hour.

- There are three **species** of zebra.

- Zebras have very good eyesight.

- At zoos, zebras can live up to 40 years.

QUICK QUIZ

1. All zebra stripes are the same.
   True or False?

2. Zebras live alone. *True or False?*

3. Zebras eat plants. *True or False?*

4. Foals stay close to their mothers.
   True or False?

GLOSSARY

Africa – the second largest continent. Kenya, Egypt, and Senegal are in Africa.

communicate – to share ideas, information, or feelings.

graze – to eat growing grasses and plants.

groom – to clean oneself and take care of one's appearance.

species – a group of related living beings.